Praise for Subhaga Crystal Bacon's Previous Books

"Crystal Bacon has a good ear. But it is clear her poems are simultaneously driven by a need to find language for feelings not easily named and the search for cooperative sounds. The combination makes for a compelling lyric authority."

> —**Stephen Dunn**, Pulitzer Prize winning author of *Pagan Virtues,* on *Elegy with a Glass of Whiskey,* BOA Editions, Winner of the A. Poulin New Poetry America Prize, 2004

"In these intimate, meticulous, compassionate poems, Bacon seamlessly marries the self with the world . . . or the human body with its love, its aging, and its griefs. With a deep mixture of curiosity and vulnerability . . . Bacon sings of our human hungers."

> —**Kenneth Hart**, author of *Uh Oh Time* on *Blue Hunger*

The poems are written in a whirlwind of forms, containing facts from public records and snippets of dialogue from the murdered victims, their loved ones, and strangers, and the details—"fingerless black gloves," "Her love for My Little Pony," that compose a life. The forms provide elegance. Dignity. The details, affinity. I tried to read Transitory as I usually approach books of poetry, but this collection asked me to supplement my reading with research. I sought news stories, faces. I wanted to know. To have known so deeply that I could feel each loss with profundity. I found myself in keeping with Subhaga Crystal Bacon, who writes, "I need to name this, the brutality of tallying the dead…not just counting, but incanting."

> —**Diane Seuss**, Pulitzer Prize winning author of *Modern Poetry,* on *Transitory*

Subhaga Crystal Bacon's brilliant new book is poetry beyond the unrelenting pressure of news cycles, giving names to harrowing statistics of murdered trans people, returning life to the air—for a moment—in the breath of a poem. When politicians sanction violence by criminalizing trans and queer bodies and branding us subhuman,

Bacon puts the love and the real live beating hearts back into their bodies, turning every No into an emphatic Yes! I love this book!

—**CA Conrad,** author of *Listen to the Golden Boomerang Return,* on *Transitory*

In Subhaga Crystal Bacon's fourth collection of poems, *Transitory,* an epigraph from Carolyn Forché instructs: "'Poetry of witness' . . . doesn't mean to write about political matters; it means to write out of having been . . . incised or even wounded by something that happened in the world" . . . Bacon stands both inside the torrent of the 44 reported deaths in this docu-poetic exploration, as she has been "incised" by the transphobia that leads to systemic violence herself, as she tells us in the opening poem, "Cautiously Watching for Violence: August 2020: the month of no murders of trans people." And she stands quietly outside as well, navigating the news for us, as witness, as eulogizer, steadily enraged.

—Review by **Julia Lisella,** *MER*

A Brief History of My Sex Life

Subhaga Crystal Bacon

LILY POETRY REVIEW BOOKS

For survivors everywhere, no matter how long it takes to know yourself. Specifically for H.

And for the healers.

To conceal all that you are. To perform your whole life / in a silence // As deep as any girlhood is; to brim over like a black pond / in summer, & say nothing about it.

Larry Levis, "Coney Island Baby"

Give me one more taste of my lost youth
And it's last call for the truth

Lucinda Williams, "Last Call for the Truth,"
Stories from a Rock N Roll Heart

Contents

Three

Before Spring Comes

Minus three this morning on the cusp of the halfway
point to spring. *Imbolc: from the belly of the mother*
where seeds begin to stir. I, too, rise

from bed, turn on the heat in my room, lift
the thermal shades to let in the light. Oxalis
leaves quiver on the shelf. In the cold air,

the smell of unlit incense from the corner altar
where I sat mornings to meditate and pray
to many-armed gods, teachers alive and dead.

I move through the house welcoming in winter.
On the sunlit hill, the raised tracks of deer,
a stitchery of life moving west across the snow.

> *I am solitary as grass. What is it I miss?*
> *Shall I ever find it, whatever it is?*

One

Creation Story

My mother always said: *I wanted all three of you,* and our birthdays—
two on the same date, different months, and one a few days prior—seemed
a sign of planning. She told us about her first husband, the virgin,
and the book they got from the minister on how to make a baby.

That brought the son she raised alone two years before she met my father.

See them there, that young woman not yet my mother and the boy tied to
a tree by his impatient aunt to play while his mother typed, sought out
among the engineers a husband to father her son. None would take
her home to meet their mothers with that inconvenient child. But then came

the one from the gas pumps, from the iron foundry, American made
with his brush cut and good intentions. So is this how we later lined
up one per season: fall, spring, winter? After the one who came before,
two more: me—neither this nor that—and a daughter. Still, I was his first.

Vintage Doll with Three Faces

As a child, I learned to know my place,
taught by a doll, who had three faces,

and a floppy body like a baby, soft
and made completely of cloth.

She had no internal organs, indeed no bones,
which is why she needed me to give her a home.

On her head, she wore a plastic hat, topped by a knob
disguised as a pompom, which turned her smile into a sob.

Rarely given what I wanted, I learned early to sob—
often in private—behind my doorknob,

no lock, no play. Once I moaned,
cradling my left arm with its broken bones.

Once for sneakers with the rubber toe over the cloth.
So much hardness when what I wanted was soft.

AAA Shame

i

Virginia, New York, Montreal—my mother
would read the little glossy AAA booklet
while my father drove and pick out

where we'd spend the night. Oh, the talk
of the differences between hotel and motel!
Once as we drove up to a lofty place

in New York State, my father said:
I can't go in there. My mother, who grew
up with all the comforts of the German

middle class—another story for another time—
said: *Our money's just as good as everyone else's.*

ii

Money. He earned it but wanted nothing more
to do with it, to know how it had been spent,
as long as the bills were paid, food on the table.

She married down, my mother. Blue collar.
So she got credit cards in different names,
took over dressing him, bringing home pants

and shirts and shoes from the local men's store.
Years, he'd come into the living room in his briefs,
shirt and pants in hand, ask: *Do these go together?*

iii

The story went that on the first day of school,
my father thought his name was Petzitillo.

Your name's Al Bacon, the teacher said.
He flushed. Not a bastard, but not legal either.

So he adopted my brother, gave him his name.
This was my father's way to undo his shame.

Self Portrait with Childhood Sex

In my neighborhood we hid,
younger kids like me,
to watch big kids
      do it
in the abandoned off-season auction.

Sometimes they would just touch
through clothes, sometimes put
their mouths on the places we knew
would feel good. Sometimes
they would go the place they called
      all the way
girls with skirts lifted

above their thighs with a sound
like crying. Later,
one would drop out of school
      in trouble
then be gone.

All I have to do is look at her

my mother bragged, proud of her parenting, the perfected *look.*
    The look that said: *Don't you dare. Don't even think about it.*
What are you, stupid? The look that froze us from across a room.
    In third grade, I went to school half days. Morning
sessions finished at lunchtime, when I did finish and didn't sit
    in the ketchup-and-milk-carton smell of the cafeteria
daydreaming instead of working. Afternoons
    walking home in that sharp Kodachrome light to watch
General Hospital. Those days she worked at the laundromat,
    scrubbing the washers, removing lint from dryers. She needed to work,
my mother—and who could begrudge her the bus ride one town over
    to wipe the machines and look over the laundry? Sometimes my father
would rescue me from the cafeteria. My father in his dungarees
    and boots and Carhartt jacket, a laborer who didn't want his wife to work.
She used to glaze over, seeing what her life would be
    if she had never married, been a *professional woman* with her little laundry
hand-washed and her apartment where she lived alone.
    We could see her there. A place where she didn't see us.

Pigeon: Symbol of Love, Loyalty, and Forgiveness

I can't remember who found it or how,
only that it was me who took it, wounded
thing, bigger than my two hands.
It had been shot with a BB gun,
dried blood on its dove grey.

In the ancient shade of Academy Street
between the elementary school
and the Methodist church,
where we used to take a shortcut,
someone found it in the grass,
a pigeon with a hole in its chest.

The walk home, across the highway,
through the field, I don't remember.
Only that my mother was there,
not working that day or at that time.
In the bathroom, she washed the wound
under the tap, holding its strong wings
close to its body, sprayed it with Bactine
that we used on our own scrapes.

Her tenderness still surprises me.

There must've been a box and paper
shredded, as we had no cage. Memory
fades here like the echo of its call.
Did we set it free one day to fly
back to its roost in the tall trees,
or did they say that to protect me
from death? It's been decades
and still I carry that wounded flight
bloody in my hands.

The Town of Broken Things

Summer mornings when I was small, I would awaken
to the auctioneer's call. Big trucks would come to haul
peppers and tomatoes, cantaloupes, peaches,
cucumbers, radishes, and scallions from Market Place.
Trees threw shade along its length, tall
already when I came along. When I was five,
I ran barefoot in hide-and-seek and leapt
with both feet around one of its trees
onto a broken Coke bottle. My neighbor, her sharp
cheekbones and upswept hair, carried me home,
bleeding on her white shorts and sandals.

Downtown was a different place, old Victorians
and shambling ancient houses, where, in early days,
glass was made from sand and fire. Later, the factory
came, Corning Glass, and three bars
in degrees of shabby. In my high school years, a *headshop*
where I walked one Saturday to meet my friend B,
who lived in the *colored section*. In a back room
lit by black lights, a poster with astrology
signs on it, Cancer, the number *69*.

I spent four years shedding my family husk
at college out by the old peach orchards.
It grew from Normal School to Teachers' College to University.
We'd hang at Nellie's Main Street Tavern and the secret
gay gathering place in Little Italy, DeFrans,
or Mazzeo's if there was a band. We'd drink beers
from sweaty pitchers. Now it's a warren of glass and chrome,
the sanitized offerings of Everytown.

There's a park in the center of my neighborhood where I broke
my arm at ten, and some kids lost their virginity
in the auction off-season. Those empty warehouses

with rows of roller conveyors. Bodies of broken
baby birds beneath the frames. There was sex
in the bushes, the basements, an outgrown playhouse. I've never
known if this was normal, happened in every town
small or large or cities where kids grow
into curiosities and desires, or if it was just us
in the buried glass and orchard runoff of home.

And Still, I Pry it Loose

My mother was a Nazi child before she came
to America(n ways), the long wearing off
of the old country: face slaps and rules
for children. All she had to do was look

at me, though she did slap first, then ask.
We were only to be seen, and when we spoke,
we used that old tongue: *Kann ich mich entschuldigung?*
to be excused from the table. Excuses,

excuses, I made my share. Up the stairs
from the dark cellar without whatever
I was sent to get. I forgot. Then her singsong
voice mocking me: *I forgahttt.* There was no back

talk. Wrong, wrong. I was harmed—
held, rubbed, touched. Was she looking then,
before time revealed the truth? With the pain,
release; with release, relief and unraveling.
I stuffed and stuffed all the words

I couldn't say, forbidden: *Who, me?*
Sunny summer child. A little slow,
they thought. But no. Not slow,
dumb from the gnarled hands that broke

something in me. Murder, murder, a sky
of claws. Black feathers, danger.
A thousand cuts. Anger, a commodity,
oil pumps in my Germanic heart.

Fat Shame

Over breakfast, I read about *Fat Eater,* the latest Shark
Tank discovery, a *totally natural and organic pill* that eats
fat. The video shows a woman in beige underwear
lifting her belly onto a tabletop. I know it's wrong.
Later in town, from the bakery came a woman
in stretchy clothes, round everywhere, carrying a cake.
Fat Eater, I thought.
                        My father's mother had a big soft body
with thin arms and legs. *Heavy* is the word we used.
So my mother warned: *You'll end up as big as mom-mom.*
When I asked for seconds at table, she would call my name
and puff out her cheeks.

I got the message. All my life, I've watched my weight—
watched it increase, my mother would say. My partner
from some years ago had a high round belly and got
an anonymous letter promoting a diet. *It really works,*
someone had written. It was her birthday. I had bought
a special cake. The letter hung in the air like candle smoke.

On TV, there's a woman whose character has *struggled
with weight* since childhood: emotional eating, body image,
and so on. How to see her life as a fight when, as I watch her
in my loose sweats, she moves like a body of water,
her beauty not lessened by her girth. Watching her,
I try to shed the shame fed to me since birth.

Mother's Braid

In her fear that after her death, we'd have
to clean up after her—

> a strand of turquoise chunks
> all the family photos
> a garnet bracelet, bound in ten-carat
> gold, with matching earrings
> sent to her from Germany.

Also:

> softening skin between chin and neck,
> impatience, her hands,
> and a crooked spine
> from which hooked parts
> ache and need to be replaced.

Mother and life and memory braided
like the one she saved, her own hair,
the one she wore wrapped around her head
> in Bavaria, cut off when she came here
> to marry a stranger at eighteen.

Like the braid she never made for me,
my hair a continent she refused to explore—
> chopped short until the year
> I begged for and got a home
> perm to roll into a flip.

> Trying in high school on my own
> to curl my hair into something
> resembling a style. She told me
> I looked like a word I refuse to write.

How deep her fear of me
> all the ways I raised myself
> all the ways she tended me.

In the picture of my mother's father,

his thighs spread, large hands on knees,
in his *lederhosen* and tall socks,
my *Opa*, trumpet player, drinker, womanizer
who scattered his seed around town.

Instead of gun and leather, I'm in denim,
carrying walking sticks, sitting on a rock.
Snow-capped mountains like his and green-black
pines. The wind sharp with cold.

He told my father that if his wife spoke to him
the way my mother spoke, he'd slap her.
My father never did, whose hands made mine.

Trumpet notes over Avalon Bay, curses about hands
that dropped what they gripped.
His genes are mystery, image, and memory.

You do not do, you do not do / Any more, black shoe

Sylvia Plath, "Daddy"

Stiff black leather, my new Doc Martens are roomy in the heel but press
on my left bunion, unpoetic part of my poet's foot. He
wore black leather boots, curled up at the ruined toes, slashed to free his own
bony growth, an eye-slit with the dingy white cornea of sock.

How he hobbled despite the shoe cut open. The pained gait. Old then,
nearly toothless, unwashed on the best of days. Rheumy-eyed when he
came to live with us, widowed. Still our grandfather. Still cruel. The music
I loved, fishwife call. My hair looked like someone threw clamshells at my head.

How vulnerable an old man can be, dying slowly from hidden
bleeds, stomach eaten with cancer, and coughing from where once were lungs.
The old Mercury with its creaking doors that took him to poker, lunch.
What he did to me and when, decades past, locked inside memory's trunk.

A Brief History of My Sex Life

At a party, in fifth grade, we decided to practice kissing.
Some of us had to be boys. I slid so comfortably
into the posture of my father on the couch, with a girl
nestled in the crook of my neck. In Scouts, I was mad
for a different girl. We camped in a house of empty rooms.
By flashlight I stroked her golden hair.

One Sunday night, in middle school, my mother ironing
in the basement, I proudly showed her my new shoes
called *Date Bait*. *What,* she said, *would you do
with a date?,* steam hissing. On and on like this
it went. Painfully dateless in high school
except for the Hop sophomore year with a boy
whose father ran a meat shop :: Junior prom,
my brother's twenty-two-year-old friend.
Senior prom :: my best friend's cousin, fresh
from the Marines, who clutched a pack of Kools
in his hairy-knuckled hands. Hooked up by God
knows who with the fey hairdresser whose mascaraed
mustache left black smears above my lip.

My brother announced that there was *just no chemistry*
between me and men. Which did not stop him
setting me up with his friends, who groped
and dry-humped me all the same. Not that I hated it.

Ever since I learned about erections, I wondered
how they stayed up. I found a device in my mother's
nightstand drawer. I imagined a sling for a soft penis.
It was a bunion stopper. The properties of blood,
how to start it, the satisfying lift and bulge, pleased me.

My first divorced fiancé wanted to wait until we married,
would press himself against my hip on parting, leave
a cum stain on my jeans. When I lost my virginity at nineteen
to the second divorced man, twelve years older than me,
I was a ready student despite the monthly fears of conception.

My mother's mother told her: *Do more than hold hands with a boy,
and you'll get pregnant, and we'll have to go drown ourselves
in the lake or your Papa will kill us.* To me, my mother said
sex was a chore, despite the way she later mourned my father.

My fiancé wouldn't go down on me, he said because
it would turn me queer. *Too late*, I should have said.
Too few the times he doled out those rare pleasures.
Confused, confused!

On the blind date disguised as an after-work party
to introduce me to the big rangy girl whose sultry voice
I loved on the corporate telephone, I said: *If I were queer,
it would ruin my life.*

But oh! How sweet her kiss in the summer night.
Drunk, we were drunk on that release! We were children
still, who lived at home. Her parents sent her away, cut
her off from what she knew. We grew up after that.
The next time I saw her, she extolled the virtues of cock.
I was broken then, some newness in me worn thin.

Wound in the Shape of a Wound I: Burning Haibun
after torrin a. greathouse

My mother / disowns me & suddenly I am a folktale. / Am I the serpent-headed girl? Or her endless / reflection? Or the winged mare burst / forth from her blood? Child of slaughter. / Wound from the mouth of a wound

She used to brag: *If you betray me,* using the indefinite you, *I flush you down the toilet.* What does it mean to disown? Somehow, though I disappointed her regularly: my hair, my legs, my weight, my clothes, my lovers. Somehow, right up to the end when I sat bedside with my sister waiting for her final breath, she did not flush me. Why? My brother, her greatest love after my father—not his father—she disowned. He did behave badly, did later hold her accountable for keeping his parentage a secret: threatening messages, letters, sending their wedding photo, a man with his face and slicked-back hair. In the will, *no provision made.* Me, the executrix, executioner with the letter informing him. What wound devoured her trust? What beast betrayed her to threaten her child with this?

*

My mother   *a folktale*
       girl

                         the mouth

of a wound

         betray

                       disappoint
       love .

               she did not   My
brother,   she disowned.   did
              keep   his parentage a secret:
                   a man with his face
and slicked-back hair.   *no provision made.* Me, the
executioner
      to threaten her child with this.

*

My mother a wound.
Betray. Disappoint. She did
disown. Threatened child.

Pantywaist. He looks like he sits down to pee.

This is what they said, with no name
for me, for what I was. Once, my mother

used the word *dyke* to describe a woman
with a cigarette dangling from her lips,

like your grandmother, meaning, I think,
a rough kind of woman.

On one prepubescent bicycle-riding day I thought:
I'll probably be a homosexual when I grow up.

Conservatives in their fear believe that
if we give them language, kids will turn out

Queer, nonbinary, or *transgender*.

They may as well burn all the dictionaries,
grow kids in silent rooms. There they'll

name themselves free.

Wound in the Shape of a Wound II

      after torrin a. greathouse

My mother   *Am I*
        her endless   reflection?   *burst forth from her*
blood?   *Wound from the mouth of a wound*

Long ago when we were already adults, my sister
sent me a birthday card that read: *For your birthday, here's
a picture of mom.* Inside, a mirror.

My father was the only one who got my mother's praise—
which he did not want—for his good looks, wavy
hair, blue eyes (weak gene we all shared)—
shapely legs. When I was five, I wore
hand-me-downs from my brother, wrangled a pair
of penny loafers. On Friday nights, we'd shop
for groceries, and I saw in my father myself. My sister
once said: *If I had everything of daddy's . . .*
and he said: *You'd be a man.*

I am not a man. Not this body,
at least. It's her body, degenerating
spine, bad joints, not lung cancer,
which killed him. It's her face, too,
in mine in every mirror, every year.
She, too, wanted to look
like her father, gypsy prince.

I found a picture of my grandmother, her heavy jaw,
straight nose, and if the dark hair were swept aside
my mother *bursts forth from her blood.*
My aunt favored their mother but with a smart mouth
slapped regularly for saying *warum*—why.
Watch and learn, my mother said: *Ja,
Papa. Danke, Papa.* Wound
from the mouth of a wound.

White dresses and poems on his name day.
My mother would be sent by her mother
to the beer hall to fetch him home for dinner.
He sang, arm slung over her child's shoulder.

She came from him. The last if you discount
the aborted son and the sons born to different
mothers. *Little Seppi, just give him a horn
and lederhosen,* they said. Seppi on the stage,
boot-shaped stein in one hand, trumpet in the other.

What is the source of this father worship?
Mothers do not suffice with their curves
and centuries of service and waiting
for everyone to go first.

For years my grandmother sat blowing his coffee
until it cooled enough to drink, while other women
bore his sons, though he made her kill their boy.
The doctor showed her his long fingers, his father's hands.

What She Said

When she asked me if I was in love
with *that girl*, nineteen to my twenty-one,
when she coaxed the truth from me one Sunday—
my father in the basement watching football,
roast in the oven, when in that wounded voice
she said: *Your daddy and I are worried*

about you. And then when I said yes,
and what relief to speak the truth,
never having the freedom to lie, to hide
(anything about myself from her prying eyes),
she said: *I'm glad you feel good about this*
now that you've ruined our lives.

She said: *It would be better if you were hooked*
on drugs. She said: *You're killing your father.*
She said: *Whoever you told this, you tell them*
that it was a mistake, and you find some man to date.
.
She put her foot down. But this, she could not forbid.
When my brother said he didn't want
that—meaning me—around his children,
she called him a *devout* I can't remember what.

Later, when she needed me to care for her in her age,
she said: *I'm prouder of you than all my children.*

For My Father

I'll take a barrel of wooden assholes if they're free. His garage orderly, sanctuary of putter and hum, alone, on a weekend. After his death, jars of fasteners arranged by size and use. Saws, hammers hung. He wasn't handy, but he was neat.

*

I put the tires up on the Buy Nothing site. The couple came in a monster truck. The kind *high as a church, homely as a house.* Maybe not safe as. One by one he tossed the tires in the bed to get a season more out of them. "Free Bird" on the stereo.

*

Smoke billows up over the empty ditch. It's not fire season, but plumes set off my adrenal system. First it smells of toast, then the hot pan, then finally, brush accelerated by gasoline. The dog and I walk the gravel bed until we meet it and see the two men, one leaning on a shovel, sent to burn what they've cut. We turn back before we're seen.

*

It's Earth Day. A trio of juncos flit and twitter in a cottonwood sapling. Have I ever heard their song this way, up close, blending both sight and sound? Junco, are you talking about the smoke or about the water coming soon? Smoke and water. Water and smoke.

*

We try not to expect the burn.

*

More and more, I think about death. I write poems that dredge up debris. What was said and done, leaving a singe.

*

My parents dead, the house that was our home (safe as) sold again. The garage might be *a barrel of wooden assholes,* an in-law suite, might be a mess of discarded junk.

Mercy

I wasn't there to sit beside him as he lay on the bed,
with my cheek on his half-empty chest, his large-
knuckled hand on my head.

My mother dosed the morphine. Maybe she gave him
a little more. That's how grief can be:
You aim where you can for relief.

The doctor said he might not die peacefully.
And he didn't. He woke to look
at my mother, naked in her love,
and took his leave.

Mal'occhio

after Jennifer Martelli

Feathers, pearls, the magic
of little grandmom
with the bowl of water,
the drop of oil,
to ward off *mal'occhio*
in my sister's youngest child.
Her secret in Sicilian
no one else could read.

Did she succeed? The baby
a woman now with a daughter
of her own, a labyrinth
of mind and heart.

The old ones die and leave
their trail of broken bowls,
the skin of oil and magic.

My Germanic people eschew
these spells. Marriage mixed
our blood. Dark hair and eyes,
but for the fussy baby's cries
missing words to remove a curse.

Du, du liegst mir im Herzen

Du, du liegst mir im Herzen.
     You, you are in my heart.
Du, du liegst mir im Sinn.
     You, you are in my mind.
Du, du machst mir viel Schmerzen.
     You, you cause me much pain.
Weiss nicht wie gut ich dir binn.
     You don't know how good I am for you.

Maybe it captures a mother's wistful lament.
Children, like lovers, unreliable recipients.

Hearing My Mother

The flowers looked like spring in the Easter display,
so I added them to my cart. Once home, unwrapped,
they drooped as if exhausted. I put them in the pitcher,
cracked and reglued but lovely still with its painted
poppies and gold trim. Flowers of sleep,
beloved of Hypnos, Nix, and Thanatos; Assyrians'
daughter of the fields. I walk the thawing earth,
revealed under melting snow pocked with autumn's
leaves. Nuthatch and chickadee come back
from wherever they've been. Tomorrow's the resurrection.
I'm not a believer with a capital B. Still,
I trust what's gone under to return. Persephone,
Jesus, even my mother, her lost voice
saying: *I can't have anything nice.*

Two

Petrichor

I came of age around water in New Jersey. Lakes,
streams, boggy ground. Dank of wet pine and soil.
An hour's drive away *the shore:* Sea Isle, Ocean City,
Margate, Avalon—we all drove its suture-like highways,
Turnpike, Parkway, Delsea Drive from the Delaware
to the Sea, Route 40 *Main Street of America* from Utah
to Atlantic City. We drove and drove, each in our own space.
Music and the dash-lights, as the night slid by greased
and shimmering as an oil spill.

Chet Baker crooned about *Moon and Sand,* the aftermath
of love, what the night had left. I heard *the smell of rain*—
familiar as the beat of my own salty blood and broken heart.
Only now, on the other side of youth, I discover: *When the night
has left us, will the spell remain?* Yes. It still carries the scent of rain.

Abecedarian of a Gender Dysphoric Childhood

As soon as I knew anything of myself, I knew that I was a
Boy, despite the ample evidence of clothing and parts to the
Contrary. I had a firm commitment to this identity:
Dressing and—within myself—being like my father at
Every turn. Weekly trips to the grocery store, always a
Family event, I wore the hand-me-down jeans and shirts
Gotten from my older brother: Johnny Tremain! and
Hung my hands from beltless loops by the thumbs.
I was sure about who I was those first ten years.
Just until puberty, when the dogma amped up, trying to
Kill off that boy in me with taunts, threats that I would
Live lonely if I stayed a tomboy. I didn't understand what they
Meant. I had plenty of friends. It was as if they thought that
Now, at the age of ten, I was someone different than I had been,
Or maybe they had changed? Anyway, I asked for a home
Perm so I could wear my hair in a flip like the beauty contestant I loved
Quietly and with deep secrecy, a kind of drag I wore
Restlessly that summer before fifth grade. Like all acts, it was
Short-lived, and by middle school, my *he* was back in secret glory,
Tomboy in navy blue blazer, my shaggy bangs and desert boots
Under the requisite dress-code skirts and jumpers. I remained a
Virgin until twenty, when I gave it up to a man
Well into his thirties. I learned from him about the importance of
Xylem, wicking moisture from root to stem. I found in tame
Yards new gardens to water, save from drought.
Zipper, I wet the world like a river.

Things in a Woman That Can Be Broken

after Jennifer Martelli

Not just the obvious, like the hymen
that breaks her girlhood when broken

Not just the perineal wall of the vagina
when she gives birth after water breaks

Not the pelvis opening to make room
for the broken egg

Spirit broken by both fist and whisper,
making her a shadow or a blade

Her voice, not the celebrated break of boys,
talked over and corrected

Not just the spirit, the voice, the parts,
woman can be broken into new, even into man

Woman wom/an wo/man w/o/m/a/n

Parsing the Nonbinary

I'm wearing a man's shirt,
man's watch and boots and belt.
My hair hangs to my waist,
my eyelids lined in a color called *rough*.

> *Rough trade:* the bodies I yearned for.
> Tongue down throat, knee between thighs.
> Is this color the come-hither look
> I use to pick out my eyes?

I've never been so confused
about who I am. My friends
used to say I was a gay man
trapped in a lesbian's body.

> *Gay*
>   *man*
>   *lesbian*
> nothing to do with *body*.

Is my body a rough
approximation of beauty
where language is silenced,
naming defunct?

        *

I thought I was a boy until puberty,
was warned that I would turn into a boy if I didn't *change*,
stop wanting a bulge in my pants.

> I was not afraid. I remember a silk blouse
> printed with elephants and mice, permed hair;
> then and later, a kind of *drag*
> as in *trial* and *disguise*.

*

A child I knew seven years ago,
who was someone's *daughter*,
under a new name, still beams
the same light as *Alex, they/them*.

> In my family, we have a child, *she/her*,
> who at seven only answered to *Finn*.
> Cut her hair, wore her brother's clothes:
> the joy of being taken for a boy.

*

I used to say: *Woman can look like this*.
And it's still true. Man, woman, female,
male, only sounds to limit what is true in us.
They, them, theirs living free in the both/and.

> It's Shakespearean; I'm a man
> disguised as a woman playing a boy.
> What a precious, private thing it is.
> She/they/them.

Protect Our Children

Slogan for Florida's anti-LGBTQ legislation

Which one arrayed behind the man with the pen
in their neat uniform will die because they
could not say *gay?* Which one holding the sign
Protect Our Children died a little bit inside
while the ink dried? Which one will run
to find kin where their true self lives?

      Which was the one shot by her father
      in Georgia? Which by his boyfriend?
      Which rests in a trash can in Chicago?
      Which was felled by the fear-fueled
       rage for being what she was, what she knew,
      despite all the laws to the contrary?

We plant shrubs and trees as the ground
thaws. Sticks with little tags
that say: *Golden Currant, Ash, Service
Berry, Maple.* They do better this way,
planted as sticks.

      Which one will dig deeply into the earth
      to send a taproot that anchors here? Which one
      in the picture, slender stick,
      will perish being planted too late?

Requiem for Girl

For Nex Benedict

Introit

The word becomes flesh
headfirst
from the canal—
introitus from the Latin—
slick with the body's
sacred waters, *vernix
caseosa*, down
on head and shoulders
if it's early,

slips into hands
gloved in white,
or into water warm
as the womb.
The cord is cut; sex
revealed, revered,
disdained. *Girl* at birth.

Kyrie Eleison

(Into the pink
the word goes,
the ribbons,
the bows.)

Lord, have mercy
upon her. Lord,
have mercy
upon her.

Unseen
the pathway
she's set on.
Rigid as
a cross
to die upon.

Lord, have mercy
upon us.

Dies Irae

Day of wrath,
                silence,
                        weeping.

Confutatis

A girl is born;
the child dies.

Lacrymosa

Weep for the child lost to the word. Weep
for pink hairbands on bald infant heads.
Weep for the boyhood forbidden to dance,
to make up his face and do his hair. Weep
for the words bound by pink and blue: tomboy,
sissy, faggot, dyke. Weep for the ones both this
and that who fight to survive, for they and them.
Weep for the ones not allowed to play, barred
from help, from health, from life. Weep
for the words that hurt. Weep, weep, weep.

I was the new thing. Then just a thing.

Diane Seuss, [Parties among strangers]

She was blond, voluptuous,
and unreliable.

I was a toy in boy's pants
and shirt, a skinny brown belt
that matched my polished shoes.

She found me cute, invited me into her bed,
where in boredom she asked:
What do you like? As if I knew.

Later I heard she said I was
a *lousy lay.*

She pretended
for years she was dying.

It's been forty years, at least.
I was nothing back then, to myself,
seeking a life in other faces, other bodies.

My Inner Johnny Mathis

A real square in my flared skirts and polyester blouses
        before I came out—after a failed engagement to a man
who introduced me to my body–the first girl I loved.

              *

Now I walk with a cane. My heartbeat's irregular.
        This morning the sun is blood-red
through smoke from fires north and south of us.

              *

Today I fed the birds, the hills through the gauze
        of burning trees still there beckoning.
Beauty recalls beauty—
I remembered Johnny Mathis,
        a neighbor's daughter
           who took me to see him at the *Latin Casino.*

              *

It was my own inner man—a little fey and feminine,
        my inner Johnny Mathis—who wanted her,
her florid color, flaming hair, freckles,
        and the deep bass note that was herself.

              *

I'm on the other coast now.
        What can I do but love
        that embarrassing youth,
alive long enough to see
        my Queer body, my changing self,
slipping like smoke through living flames?

In Memoriam of Past Rain

Once I spent a frigid weekend
in a dank, unheated room

in Atlantic City's Hotel Byron
back before casinos pushed

out the indigent veterans
of many wars. (Memorial Day,

parades of the old in uniform,
their peaked hats over solemn faces,

walking or wheeled, the last
surviving soldier from this war

or that, flags of cloud, bullets
of drizzle.) In the mildewed room,

a woman I taught to find her clitoris
and orgasm. That war she fought

within herself. What country she claimed.
Old, old now, this remembering.

A lost name. A slim, almost childlike body
locked against the knock of pleasure.

The beckoning street, the salty, rain-
drenched night slick with broken light.

Soft Spot

for Chris

Resting on its nest of thighs, its nest
of eggs, his soft dick. The only way
I ever saw it. My long-dead friend, his cupid's
body, his concupiscence at odds with his innocence:
nude at home, the fluid silk of kimono,
the limp wrist, and Player's smoke. His languid
eyes and droll mouth. His lazy words.

Nights he and his friend, Donald, would go out
looking for Richard, they would say. Calling
on Spruce Street: *Richard, Richard!* Only
to find him, as ever, at the bath house,
where they competed for a pink plastic pig—
trophy—whoever had the most men that night.

That last year when we shared a townhouse,
the crazy trick-cum-boyfriend who said he
was a warlock and whose teeth could be removed,
leaving a frightful hole in his face, called
the fire trucks on us. A parting threat (not the fire
but the sirens) after he had beaten my friend
with a vacuum cleaner hose, of all things.

Later, we traded massages. Him naked on my back,
on my buttocks. The soft of him like a purse
spent of coin. His penis relaxed, almost feminine,
delicate, stripped of its hot blood, its one
eye closed for now to what might be gotten.

Husbandry

I used to think I wanted a husband, a soft
cushion against the world's sharp corners.
Like that least husband-material jazz

pianist, my friend's brother, who once lifted
the sheets for me to back into his belly.
A husband like a brother, like my friend Paul,

who used to drag me down Christopher Street,
me in one hand, bagged tall boy
in the other. Thomas, whose bed I shared

for mostly chaste naps before the baths
for him and a book for me. Now I am
husband to myself, that deep drop

into the root of me; the daily chores:
dog watcher in the still dim morning
when hungry things might lurk. Fire-maker,

wood mover, tea boiler. I'm self-
anointed in baggy sweats and men's vest.
Never mind my breasts, soft vent,

the place that opens to where I'm cleft.

All I Need to Know

My voice changed when I was twenty-two
from a long overdue tonsillectomy. Before that,
though, I would play the dulcimer, badly, and sing
Shady Grove and *Charlie's Neat*, songs
I learned from a girl I loved but couldn't have
when we were camp counselors one summer.

The old professional feminists from my school
used to gather on Sundays to Consciousness Raise,
and I brought the dulcimer and the throaty voice
they said they'd listen to if I *read from the phone
book*. But I brought more, brought poems, brought songs,
brought bright star to their grey doves.

Now I feel that vague longing for vibrant youth,
untouched, just the thirst-slaking gaze and flush.
Spring's choked my vocal cords. Young bodies
float like pollen on the breeze.

Venus Dreaming

It's still pleasing to my eye, this aging sack of pain.
Still rosy, stained with ink winding up my arms,
a fading story etched in skin. Shoulder-cup bear,
lotus, snake of Sanskrit twined in leaves. The Great Wave
splashing over a form of my name, *Om Subhagayai
Namaha,* invoking the Divine. The Mother.

I gaze and gaze like Narcissus in his pool. Lovely boy,
so lovely, a flower, perhaps a fool. I, too, am lovely.
Hair pulled back, my face unlined. I am neither mother
nor boy. I wear this body: breasts meeting belly
rounded under ribs. This mound of Venus dreaming.
I'm not a flower, not transformed by my own gaze,
the reflecting pool broken by the crashing wave.

Pride

In the picture, under the striped flag,
two young women with pink hair
wear plunge-neck crop tops over
golden bellies. One wears white so sheer
her nipples appear like those candies, *Capezzoli
di Venere,* Nipples of Venus. I, too,
once bared my belly, even, in summers,
my breasts baked brown by Fire
Island sun where nakedness was prized
and the simple walk to grocery shop,
a meat market, everyone appraised.

That was another life of profligacy,
tight butt, reliable hips, the feast
of heat on hungry skin. Today
my cane dangles from my wrist,
a broken wing until I grasp it, then—
like a creature from a myth—transformed
into an extra limb, conveys superpowers
like walking pain-free from A to B.

On Philandering

I've been thinking about the word *philanderer*
that we use to mean a notorious flirt and seducer
of women. Yet our roots and prefixes firmly fix

phil, love, to *ander*, man. I once learned a supposed
Greek saying: *For practice a sheep, for pleasure a boy,*
for children a woman. I don't know if that's true,

but men who love men are philanderers. *Homophile*
switched sex with love, and in French, *mattachine*
were men who danced masked to poke fun at society.

Gertrude Stein gave us *gay. Miss Furr and Miss Skeene*
were quite regularly gay though one left the other behind.
But before that, so carefree in their love, were Miss Furr

and Miss Skeene. So gay! More carefree than, say,
the Daughters of Bilitis, a fictional friend of Sappho,
who loved girls and lived on Lesbos, so, you know,

all who live on Lesbos are Lesbians, just not gay.
I've been thinking about philandering the way
the implicit man might meet the implicit woman
in the same body. That would be so regularly gay!

Night in Winnemucca, NV

Helene has a broken ankle and a scooter. Her staff's got COVID. The lobby's full of unmasked men. Helene's got a brusque, business-like flirt. The bedside lamp's out, plug buried behind the immovable bed screwed into the wall. My cheesesteak and fries sweat after the slow check-in, the lamp debacle, refusing the masked maintenance man who came to rummage in the bedclothes, fix the light. After the soggy sandwich and two beers, I unscrew a bulb from the desk lamp by the door to try beside the bed. I text Helene in her room off the lobby: *Presto! It's fixed.* I stretch out on the bed, feet freed from twelve hours of boots, joints loosed from the long day's drive north and home. Leonard Cohen's *Chelsea Hotel* repeats in my mind: *I need you. I don't need you, and all of that jiving around.* No one's *giving me head.* The light shines on the stiff spread, curtains luff in the window unit's heat. Construction trucks beep into the frigid masculine night.

Communion

This is my body,
which I'm giving to you.

> These twin scars on my right thigh,
> skin like melted glass, rivers of cooled lava.

> This new hip, that opens, lifts to wrap
> its leg around you. Take this grey
> sacral hair. Climb into, enter me with care.

This is my blood,
> freshly thinned
> by daily drugs,
> pumped through
> my chemically slowed heart,
> its palpitations nothing to do with you.

Take, eat, for this is my body.

Drink of me, the scents
of well-worn places,
elixir of longing living,
lived in.

After Reading Saeed Jones' *Prelude to Bruise*

There's a body within a body. One is woman;
one is man. There's a spell in words that stir
these layers, blur what's real. Naked beneath
a linen dress, refuge from heat—from waist-
band, belt—a tent of thread and air. I'm stirred,
stirring, nipples exhale. Below my navel—
tides rise and fall, hard and soft with blood—
what to call the place that's both inside and out?
I dream as I read that I have been in that stall,
that bed, felt the thrusts, the cracked open jaw,
the throat, the ass. Have I dreamed these scenes?

The throat, the ass. I have dreamed these scenes:
that bed, felt the thrusts, the cracked open jaw.
I dream as I read that I have been in that stall—
what to call the place that's both inside and out—
tides rise and fall, hard and soft with blood.
Stirring, nipples exhale; below my navel,
banned belt, a tent of thread and air. I'm stirred.
A linen dress, refuge from heat, from waist,
these layers blur what's real. Naked beneath:
one is man. There's a spell in the words that stir.
There's a body within a body. One is woman.

Small Triggering Sign

They called him *Joe the Rug*, because of his last name and his hair.
He was a bullish boy, though to me he was more like a man, 18 to my 15.

>They said he'd raped a girl. My mother said he was not so ugly
>that he'd have had to force her. That was how we saw it then,

boys and men taking what was not given. A nicely carved wooden sign
outside a fenced yard brought back his name. I won't write it.

>When as a college junior I applied to substitute teach,
>the superintendent ended the interview saying:

We need more clean young women like you. He didn't know
that I was unclean, a woman who savored the sex

>of other women. New to it as I was. I asked my first lover:
>*How did I do?* How we rubbed ourselves on each other,

scissored legs to join our soft, wet parts.
A nice clean young woman. What he meant was white, I'm sure,

>and straight. In childhood, my mother said one day:
>*You need to use this,* handing me deodorant.

And later, at Girl Scouts, the leader said: *Someone smells
good.* I said it was me, that I was wearing deodorant.

>The other day, my partner and I compared how often we shower,
>our skin so thin and dry here in the high desert. Her name means the sweet

smell of Shiva. It's true; she smells sweet, always, even her sweat
which, back in the day, was profuse on the disco floor. Holding me,

freshly showered, before I went to town, she said: *You smell good.*
I'm past the age for sex, though it dies slow, the libido.

Mine still runs the loop from time to time,
imagining this or that body in my naked embrace.

But they're more like trailers than films, short
with all the good stuff front-loaded. Sometimes, my mind

is a Potemkin Village—all the people gone, replaced
by actors who live their real lives within the fake.

Queer Shame

[T]he "queer" label might refer to those persons whose sense of identity is most enduringly structured by shame.

affectsphere

i

Slapped hands
in a bright room. The hands mine,
the slap my mother's.
                    There was light
and the familiarity of my body,
or beyond—maybe before—my body,
self. I went on touching
            through the years in beds,
closets, basements   come
from another's wrong touch.

ii

The Editor erased me.
        She calls me *she,* erasing *they,*
which she does not like.

iii

most enduringly, not endearingly,
structured by shame. Old now,
my structure cracks.
        My pronouns shift
beneath its weight. Correctness,
grammar, agreement. I disagree.

iv

Can you see me now? Shining out
from the breaks, hands resting
        wherever they land,
            like over-wintering birds
            hungry, flashing in the light?
I touch myself, rough or soft
            as fresh snow on naked limbs.
Pure. A love in unique parts.

Poem for My (Non-Existent) Adult Child

You were not conceived, despite the spent seed,
the rich bed of blood. You did not fill my arms
with bittersweet. No tears from midnight
dreams, fevers. Your body made of mine,
my mother's chin. Your gender your own, *selfness*.
You love who and what you love. You are
a pearl of the world, gem of grit and spit,
that gives you a shell and a tongue both salty
and sweet. We speak once a day or week.

I did you right and wrong from my own pocket
of wounds and stars. Fleet as the scent of mock
orange on the wind, you are a blossom of loss,
phantom limb.

All that blue

This morning, I washed the earthenware teapot,
its spout cracked under the glaze, worn down by accidental
smacks against the porcelain border between sinks. I used

to let it sit till dinner, a second cup of tea
my ritual, sometimes after breakfast while I wrote,
or later in the day when my energy slacks like a wet

flag from its pole. Or like the twisted lilac, listing north,
its heart-shaped leaves against the morning sky
brown with freeze. Brown like the pot

deep, circular vessel . . . drinking cup.
The spout a lip, my lip a cup to drink
the tannin-stained tea I gave up to save

my heart, *a spout bursting through all that blue.*

Three

Penumbra

Moon dial, stake thrust into my vampire's heart.
Innocent predator, despoiled child
with a hunger I could not name or satisfy:

This is the behavior of children
who've been sexually abused.

Images escape from the rim of sunspot,
memory burrowed in the darker core.

What if *I* am the light? Decades long elliptic
spun within like Saturn's rings. Lingering
winters broken by brief glimpses
of what the sun has shown me.

After the Psilocybin Journey, I Remember (Precis)

A skull head with screws for teeth

    toes curled and his fingers
        bent so far, they were invisible

A red and black room
        velvet curtains, a carousel horse

A charge of pleasure
        then shame

Interlude

After poetry's pâté-rich pages,
slender spines, I need a sturdy plot.
A palate cleanser, usually.

I read a book by an Irishman.
Self-effacing, overly self-conscious
characters—nobody who they appear to be.

Then a priest gets whacked, his gear cut off.
The skein of harm, vindictive
as it was, a crime. When the dead man

speaks close to the book's end
it's called *an interlude* in which he
tells us how he loved his work

with orphan boys. How he committed
the sin of the special relationship
with a boy he calls Ginger, a big boy

though only nine. How he would *love*
the boy after mass, despite his cries.
How he would flog the boy when bad,

then comfort him. On it goes, rape
upon rape. Never mind the priest's
own childhood. A father who came

at night with a pocketful of sweets
to forge a secret with his son.
I've got my own wound, still fresh

around the edges to any unexpected
poke. I'm not a story, a fiction.

Still, reading this, I knew the boy

he fucked for years until the man
he became took up the shears.

Grandfather

You are a ghost town from another country:
store signs unreadable, illegible, paint worn
down to cracked wood beneath. Dust scents
the air here. It makes me sneeze. Still,
I press into your empty streets. Shoes
echo on the fading macadam. I wear boots
like you, laced up, martial in peacetime.
Black, the leather a little broken over bone
growths. Is it garlic I smell? Your breath,
or am I making that up? Your body
unwashed. Your hands unusable. Joints
unbendable. The mark you left, invisible
ink only I can see in a language I cannot read
or have forgotten.

Psilocybin-Recovered Memory

I am the yarn of my own remaking,
        shades of purple bled out
to what's stored and well-buried under years.

Where my body is bone of hip and pubis,
        muscle and tissue, only space
between my navel and my thighs.

The trouble spot erased, an open
        keyhole of faces—a series of shuttlecocks—
to sweep colors back and forth until,

        as Rembrandt said of his nudes: *I want
to pinch*. And I did not pinch but swept
        my hands between my hips and thighs

to find my lap affirmed
        and firm with flesh. Like a key in a forgotten lock,
it turned me toward a glint of light,

        ruffle of dress, and the lap of the man
who raised my father. And then heat
        and suffocation beneath the comfort

of weighted blanket, flailing arms.
        The watcher asks: *How are you doing?*
I say: *Something happened.* On his lap,

        where I am told I loved to climb,
couldn't get enough, he touched me,
        or something in me touched in him

what he couldn't or didn't resist.
        I can't be more clear. I was only three.

Or, if not three, then two, walking.

No words for what happened, only fear
flowering in my flesh.
No longer only seed.

In Which I Begin to Understand

my sex that sought heat and friction
to bloom, that took me to slapped hands,
to a child's touch, a boy-penis

its smell of warm skin, a dark
closet where he let me touch it, touched
mine, girl's small nub,

all my after-years, it led my sex,
clitoris lit like a bulb.

In all my fumblings, the urgency
to come, a fuse lit
when I was too young.

I would say he broke me then, or left me
this splinter with its slow path:
sixty-seven years. I pull it out. Clean.

The Weight of Words

Layers of words over sixty years like the paint on every
        piece of furniture in my grandmother's home, each one rescued from junk
by my grandfather, my un-doer. Paint, thick, brown, and in one case
        pink with Q-tip swirls of gold that chipped away like nail polish to bare

tin. A month past the recovered memory, a hole opened. I slipped—
        not through—just far enough to be intimate with the dark where I hung,
a spider on silk that couldn't hold, re-spun out
        of myself, thread between living and dying.

Words to harm, limit, wound, and words to uncover a wound.
        I spoke my fear at last to my sister, my remaining family:
that I would be disowned. Named that vulnerability. From my tin-
        man's chamber scraped clean of what obscured me—

under the glossy surface, slick with oil and pigment to hide damage—
        words I write, words I've written, words that spool out of me, a lifeline.

Eagle Heart Sanctuary, Olympia, WA

Holes cut in the platform around the tree trunks. Tall, tall Doug firs move in the breeze, and this solid sturdy floor, former treehouse floor, creaks and sways. The earth and everything on it moving.

*

Sticky white sap like glue, like cum, runs in the jigsaw bark. Dots the floor with its needle litter, brown, twiggy, and tiny spent pollen cones. Maple keys. A squirrel's trash heap of picked-over seed cone scales like dried petals. A zipline runs from here across the woods a few hundred feet.

*

What a childhood E's daughter had here! Wild and safe.

*

Holes in childhood. Holes in platforms whole kids could drop through. No one watching our hidden touching. Or holes in those who watched where whole childhoods fell through.

*

There's a hole through a wooden disk for a rope to pass. Up and up it goes to an unseen branch. At the bottom a loop for a step. Or a neck.

*

I drove across the country. I drove to this peninsula with its outsized trees and sword ferns, banana slugs with bodies like uncut cocks, with the mantle and the optical tentacles that retract. Undulant, moving six and a half inches a minute in their trail of slime. I came all this way, to leaf mold and trillium. To mushrooms grown for medicine. Under the trees. I traveled back two decades an hour.

*

In the warp and weft of music, I was rebuilt, I found the hole in myself between navel and thighs. And saw the human shuttlecocks that wove me back until I was whole. My body a mass of earth and whistle of breath.

*

After three hours, death's head came, a skull with teeth of six-inch screws, a double row of screws, screws falling from its hideous jaw. I glimpsed my toddler self and my father's father, his toothless smile, and my body burnt and restrained, then I ugly cried. Something *had* happened ~~in my couldn't-get-enough clambering on him~~ in my frilly dresses on his junkman-filthy lap.

Singing Bowls

I stood in the deep bronze bowl. Put my feet
on the feet engraved there while the guide
rang its vibrato into the core of me: root, sex, power,
plexus, heart, throat, and out the top of my head.

Just now, a late wasp, November first, hums
from closed window to closed window. With a broom,
I coax it out the door, brown body flickering
in afternoon light. Sitting in this cabin, its stilt
legs under the back deck, hand-sized leaves rain
down onto the failing wood. The trees create
a woody bowl. Somewhere across the way
someone hammers throughout the day. At night,
two owl voices build in the dark.

Context: In Which I Retreat to My Family Tree

I line up all the photos I culled to bring
on this retreat in the woods. Me at two weeks,
then in a dress with a wide white skirt.
How can a five-year-old show such defeat?

Here are my father's parents at their youngest son's
wedding. They're old and small, poverty and death
disguised in blue satin, black tux.

There's my mother's father in his fancy shorts
and vest, triumphant on stage. His outstretched arms
clasp his trumpet, a beer glass the size and shape
of a boot. His wife wears traditional Bavarian
clothes, has my mother's mouth.

My parents on vacation in the Fatherland. In one hand,
my dad's cigar, arm around my mother's waist.
Her pointy breasts and permed hair. She'd painted
her nails bright red, which my father didn't like
but seems to have allowed.

Some birthday of mine, three or four. In pigtails,
I sit on my godmother's lap, bare-chested
against her bandeau-clad breasts. My godfather's
shirt open. Early summer. We all sweat.

This is an altar: faces unleashed, burnt
candles, a pint bottle of rye. A cleft
rock I found on a walk as the remembrance
of what was done to me came on.

Outside, leaves stack up in piles of red,
gold, and brown. A branch strikes the wall,
shows me there's nothing here to fear.

Last night so many knocks on roof and beam,
I barred the door. No rustle in the leaves,
no footfall. In daylight, nothing amiss.
I'm aloft in the branches of trees
fragrant with the season's spent end.

I came back because there was nowhere else to go.
after Anne Sexton

Rain pings the tin roof.
All the work of men done for a day,
a small fire in the stove kills the damp.
I'm inside the nearly naked trunks of trees.
Their sodden, long-dead leaves surrender
like ghosts to waiting earth. I admit,
I sized up boughs perpendicular—
is there not an easier word?—to the ground.
Slim, muscular as the arms of young men,
just a knowing, here's where I could string
myself up. Stump nearby. I really
have no wish to die.

Naming and Claiming

Another sleepless night after the long slow train
with its intermittent whistle, the last one of the day
at 11:15. It calls forth the chorus of yard dogs
scattered over the far hill. They, too, must hear
the wild movements in the noisy leaves.

They call out: *Who goes who goes who goes*
and *I'm here I'm here I'm here*. Deer afoot!
Foxes! Rabbits! Like them, I rise to the sounds
of trespass—ha! I'm the intruder here
in my house on stilts—to look out in the full
moon light for whatever stirs. I *know* there's no harm
to me, big two-leg with my human stink, my headlamp
that picks out frightened eyes at ground level. Still.
At last, it's the owl, one I heard pick off some prey,
the landing and then each feather's swoop in under-
brush. Later contentedly cooing its unmistakable *hoo*—

Who, indeed. I wake so vulnerable and, let's face it,
homesick. I've been away almost two weeks already,
not just in distance but into the depths of early wounding.
Memory is a chimera. What's buried in the mind
dwells quietly in the body. What I recalled of trespass
against my innocence has little content, yet nudges me
in its awakening to bring me, too, awake; vigilant.

Even in the lunar light, a rural road, few homes,
even in that safety, we're here: to write and
keep to ourselves. Even in trees—*trees!*—
my lifelong companions and friends, there's
if not fear then alertness to what harm is possible
on this farm, this road, this land with its history of loss.

And in loss, we know love. *Love is the love of who we are,*
it is a form of knowing. And now I am the love for what I lost.

Writing Residency in Tennessee

Hours of heavy equipment grinding, hidden
by trees noisily dropping hand-shaped leaves.

I'm fighting off or surrendered to a cold I get
every time I travel, or it's the malaise of coming to know
and saying the words: *I was sexually abused.*
Wondering if anyone will believe me.

*

When my grandfather was dying, I was sent to meet the surgeon
to learn the results of his biopsy. He asked: *Where
are your parents?*

        Later when my father
came home hot and tired from eight hours
bolting up beams, I said: *It's not good news.*
And he said, not kindly: *I can take it*, while
prying off his boots, toe to heel. His mother
already dead. That man, his stepfather who'd
raised him since infancy, living out his limited
time with us.

        What did I know? His last days,
my mother tried to shame me to his hospital room
where he labored while she worked. Where the resident,
they later said, told him gently: *Not long now, Chief,*
in the days when you might use the word that way.

*

All I can say is it came to me, this truth, after years
of clues. I needed help. I got it. I'm older now.
Old enough to wonder about his life. Sicilian.
Immigrant. Secret speaker of mother tongue.

Once he told me my hair looked like someone had thrown
clam shells at my head. He mistook satire
on TV for real—two men in that ad that said:
My wife, I think I'll keep her—Geritol.

Two homos! he said, outraged while we played
rummy, my sister and me and him. New Year's
Eve, 1975, the year before he died.

He was dead by the time I came out.
Driving his '63 Mercury I'd painted
taxicab yellow into a VW bug head-on
in slow motion, dreaming of a girl
who would break my heart.

*

A train's gone by, leaving its mournful sound,
the machinery in the woods quiet now.
Quitting time. We're all working on something,
tearing up the ground.

Self Portrait at the End of a Season

Two hours until sunrise, a crown of oak
is etched against a pewter sky.
So long since I've walked in leaves,

their garrulous warning to the listening world:
Someone's coming! Acorns ping
and rattle, roll along the cabin's

roof. Late last night, foxes barked.
One nearby, the other answering
from across the way.

I saw faint window lights through trees
but no watching, wild eyes.
Here they are again! Their yips

ring in the hillside above a hum
of far-off cars. In Cape Breton
once, at a place called World's End,

at dusk a litter of kits wrestled
in the road, a knot of red coats,
by a sheer drop to the North Atlantic.

I'm a long way from that memory
and home, wherever that may be.

Pro-nominal

After Maggie Nelson's *Bluets* and *The Argonauts*

Maybe it's the dark-wash denim
and navy shirt so midnight on my skin,
the way they make a rippled pool
on a chair. How my eyes flare cobalt
against my sunlit hair. Naked,
I lay face down in floral sheets.
The slow, healing strokes of the oiled
arm pressing, pressing me down.
My breasts flatten, disappear,
no longer woman, not man.
Crescent scars, pectoral moons,
healed blue gills to breathe.
In this state, my body's a clean slate,
and the word—*they*—sings like blue
whales' song of home
that calls me—safely—blue, to *them*.

If I give you my heart, will you promise
not to break it?

Green leafy bush behind her head, the intuitive sat
before her San Diego window, one curled vine
waving in the blast of sunlight. She sensed
my young self, the age of my wounding,
with its deep sadness and righteous rage.

> The child wants to be called Subhaga, not Crystal,
> name given to her because someone else had given it
> to *their* daughter, *the most beautiful thing she could think of.*
> A hand-me-down story and name, nothing to do with her.
> Child without words, who came into life *to be loved*
> *by women, to be in sisterhood, a lifelong seeking.*

Inside me, my child-self fights for this love
down to the final years. At nearly seventy,
she's ready to blossom out of the rift they left.

The Book Speaks

I cannot put my memories in order.
The moon just wrecks them every time.
Marosa Di Giorgio, *The History of Violets, XVIII*

I am a jaw pried open,
old barber's pole red
and white striped, rough tools,
a little blood and pain. Then
release. Who needs Novocain?
A hit of bourbon. Quiet room.
Trees with their promise of relief: hung.
Jung said tooth loss means transition.
Beyond transitory, evolving.
I'm the place you come to unlock
what time and your mind buried
so deeply, you had to travel
the mycelium highway to reach it.
Here I find you. Innocent.
Vessel of shame and rage.
I open you. Unbutton your genes.
You are warrior. Let loose your hair.
Take up the space you crave.
Now, do you see?
You can love what you are
without flinching.

Acknowledgements

My sincerest thanks to editors who published sometimes earlier versions of these poems in the following journals:

45th Parallel, "Husbandry"

Action, Spectacle, "Pantywaist. He looks like he sits down to pee."

Anti-heroin Chic, "I came back because there was nowhere else to go."

Bellevue Literary Review, "Mercy" (formerly "When I Wasn't There")

Beyond Queer Words, "After Reading Saeed Jones' *Prelude to Bruise*"

Braving the Body, "Fat Shame"

Diode, "Petrichor"

Down the Stairs, "All that blue"

Ghost City Press, "Night in Winnemucca, NV"

Hare's Paw Literary Journal, "Soft Spot"

Indianapolis Review, "Naming and Claiming"

Mom Egg Review, "Mother's Braid"

MUSE Literary Journal, "All I have to do is look at her"

Naugatuck Review, "A Brief History of My Sex Life"

Nixes Mate, "What She Said"

Paterson Literary Review, "Before Spring Comes," "Singing Bowls"

Pirene's Fountain, "Self Portrait with Childhood Sex," "Wound in the Shape of a Wound I"

Pure Slush: Growing Up Lifespan Vol. 2: "Abecedarian of a Gender Dysphoric Childhood"

Quartet Journal, "If I give you my heart, will you promise not to break it?"

Querencia, "Venus Dreaming"

Queerlings, "In Memoriam of Past Rain"

River Heron Review, "Pro-nominal"

Sangam, "Mal'occhio"

San Pedro River Review, "Vintage Doll with Three Faces"

scissors & spackle, "The Town of Broken Things"

Smartish Pace, "Parsing the Nonbinary"

Solstice Poetry Review, "Requiem for Girl"

SWWIM, "For My (Non-Existent) Adult Child"

Unbroken, "For My Father, A Zuihitsu"

Wordpeace, "Pride," "On Philandering," "Communion"

"And Still, I Pry It Loose" and "Parsing the Nonbinary" were included in the *Washington State Queer Poetry Anthology;* "And Still, I Pry It Loose" and "All I have to do is look at her" are forthcoming in the anthology *The World We See: Women Poets on Neurodivergence* from Texas Review Press.

Author's Notes

This book would not have been possible without the help of many wonderful people and opportunities. My partner, Sugandhi, helped me unpack the ways I, like most of us, was shaped by both my family and the culture in which I was raised. Her support has been immeasurable. My family has been a gift of sustenance. My writing group, the irreplaceable Pretzels, including *The Queen of Queens,* my friend, the late Jennifer Martelli, friends, Brandel France de Bravo, and Barbara O'Dair. My local writing group, the Confluence Poets, and early reader, Emily Warn. My friend, the therapist EK, for the powerful psilocybin journey and integration work. Sundress Academy for the Arts, where I wrote the third section of the book. Eileen Cleary's insightful line edits made each poem the best it could be. Like the psilocybin, they pared away what obscured the greater truths. And to Diane Seuss, who said "I am who and what made me," thanks for your work. It gave me permission to write this.

The poem "Before Spring Comes" includes a line from Sylvia Plath's "I am solitary as grass." The poem "All that blue" contains a line from Ellen Bass' "Ever Changing Song." In "Naming and Claiming," the lines, "Love is the love of who we are, / it is a form of knowing," are from "Komodo" by Sharon Olds. *If I give you my heart, will you promise not to break it?* is from Lucinda Williams' "I Lost It." "For My Father" includes a line from Elizabeth Bishop's "The Moose." The poem "Petrichor" has a line from and references the poem "The Sacred" by Stephen Dunn.

About the Author

Subhaga Crystal Bacon (they/them) is the author of five collections of poetry. In addition to *A Brief History of My Sex Life*, they include the Lambda Literary finalist, *Transitory*, 2023, winner of the BOA Editions, Ltd. Isabella Gardner Award for Poetry; *Surrender of Water in Hidden Places*, winner of the Red Flag Poetry Chapbook Prize, 2023, released in an expanded second edition in the summer of 2024; *Blue Hunger*, 2020, and *Elegy with a Glass of Whiskey*, winner of the A. Poulin New Poetry America Prize from BOA Editions, 2004. A Pushcart and Best of the Net nominee, Subhaga is an AWP Writer to Writer mentor and teaching artist working in schools and libraries with youth and adults, as well as private students. A Queer elder, they live with their partner, the painter, Sugandhi Katharine Barnes, and their Labradoodle, Lola, in rural north central Washington on unceded Methow land.